WOW!
Look what's in the
Oceans

KINGFISHER
LONDON & NEW YORK

Copyright © Macmillan Publishers International Ltd 2019
Published in the United States by Kingfisher,
120 Broadway, New York, NY 10271
Kingfisher is an imprint of Macmillan Children's Books, London
All rights reserved.

Distributed in the U.S. and Canada by Macmillan,
120 Broadway, New York, NY 10271
Library of Congress Cataloging-in-Publication data has been applied for.

Author: Camilla de la Bédoyère
Design and styling: Liz Adcock
Cover design: Liz Adcock
Illustrations: Ste Johnson

ISBN: 978-0-7534-7517-1 (HB)
ISBN: 978-0-7534-7518-8 (PB)

Kingfisher books are available for special promotion and premiums.
For details contact: Special Markets Department, Macmillan, 120 Broadway, New York, NY 10271

For more information, please visit
www.kingfisherbooks.com

Printed in China
9 8 7 6 5 4 3 2 1
1TR/0119/WKT/UG/140WFO

WOW!
Look what's in the
Oceans

KINGFISHER

LONDON & NEW YORK

Oceans are BIG!

All five oceans, and about 20 seas, are connected to each other and create the World Ocean.

There are five huge areas of salty water on the planet. They are called oceans and together they cover 70 percent of Earth's surface. That's why we call our home the Blue Planet!

Atlantic Ocean

I'm a giant squid.

Sailing all around the world takes at least 40 days!

I'm an ocean sunfish.

Pacific Ocean

Wow!

Salty water makes a great home for animals. The largest squid are bigger than a bus, but the smallest ones are tinier than your thumbnail!

I'm a walrus

Arctic Ocean

Guess what?

There are vast mountains and volcanoes beneath the seas. Some are so deep in places that even Mount Everest—the tallest mountain on land—would disappear beneath the surface!

The oceans hold about 679,000,000,000,000 bathtubs full of salty water. That's 679 trillion!

Pacific Ocean

Indian Ocean

We are clown fish.

whose tail is this?

Southern Ocean

I'm a king penguin.

Focus on fish

The oceans are home to billions of fishes, which come in all shapes and sizes!

Butterfly fish look like butterflies, parrot fish have beaklike mouths, and pineapple fish look like pineapples!

which do you think I am?

I'm an oarfish and I'm realllllly long!

An oarfish looks like a long, silvery ribbon and measures up to 50 feet (15 meters) long!

Wow!

Many fish use venom to sting their prey, or to defend themselves. Electric fish have a different super power—they zap other animals with a big electric shock!

Titan triggerfish don't like people! If something or someone gets too close to a titan triggerfish, they may get bitten or walloped by a mighty tail.

Thwack!

oww!

Freaky-looking frogfish open up their giant mouth and suck in their prey faster than a vacuum cleaner!

we're in a big school!

I'm cleaning up!

Wow!

A big group of fish is called a school, and swimming together helps fish avoid attacks from hungry predators. A single school of silvery herring can contain more than 10 million fish!

Long-distance swimmers

Travel through the oceans with these awesome explorers.

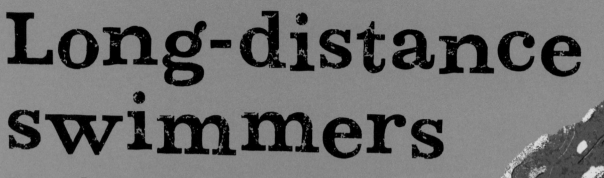

There's a great reward in store for a hungry gray whale. This big beast swims 5,000 miles (8,000 kilometers) to reach the Arctic Sea, where it feasts on 77 tons of food during the summer!

Where's my dinner?

Slow down, kids!

Blue shark moms swim across the Atlantic Ocean before giving birth to up to 50 babies!

Wow!

Spiny lobsters hold onto each other as they march across the seabed in a long line!

A long animal journey is called a migration. Animals migrate to find food or mates, or safe places to have their young. The world's longest migrations all take place at sea.

Slow and steady wins the race!

One record-breaking leatherback turtle swam an incredible 12,773 miles (20,556 kilometers) across the world's oceans.

Are we nearly there yet?

Eels trek an epic 3,000 miles (5,000 kilometers) across the Atlantic Ocean. They swim the whole way without eating or resting!

Left, right! Left, right! 9

Dive into the forest

Join super-cute sea otters in a lush green paradise.
But watch out for what's lurking underneath . . .

There are huge forests growing under the water. Made of giant kelp, these forests are home to many animals, including sea otters.

I'm a Sea urchin and I eat the kelp— yum!

Wow!

A single kelp plant can be 213 feet (65 meters) long, and it grows up to 18 inches (46 centimeters) a day! Kelp is a type of seaweed, or algae, that grows only in salty water.

I'm a Sea otter and I eat sea urchins!

Algae and other sea plants help our planet's health by making oxygen. It's the gas that humans and other animals need to breathe to stay alive!

I'm fishing for fry!

In warm places, where the land meets the sea, mangrove trees grow. Their long roots make a perfect hiding place for crocodiles and other animals.

Baby fish are called fry. We're hiding from scary crocs!

Wow!

Sea beasts called dugongs and manatees live near the shore, where they eat seagrasses. They pop their heads above water to breathe. People have mistaken them for mermaids!

Wonderful whales

These mighty mammals are clever, strong, and precious.

Dolphins and porpoises are related to whales but they're much smaller—only 10 feet (3 meters) long. The largest whales are 33 times longer and 3,000 times heavier!

I'm blowing my nose!

Danger!

A quarter of all types of whales and dolphins are in danger of dying out forever. In the past, humans hunted thousands of whales every year, but now most countries protect them.

Whales can stay underwater for more than an hour, but they come to the surface to breathe. The blowholes on top of their heads are nostrils!

Hello up there!

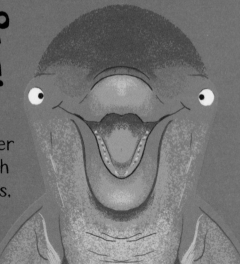

Whales and dolphins are clever animals that can talk to each other with deep booming calls, clicks, or whistles.

Incredible killer whales are so clever they can plan attacks on their prey! They work in teams to knock seals off ice floating in the sea.

Surprise!

Uh oh!

Wow!

Whales are mammals, which means they give birth to their babies and feed them with milk. Mothers teach their babies how to find food and stay safe.

Can you hear singing?

Hey mom, watch me spurt water from my blowhole!

13

Brrr . . . it's icy cold

Explore the mysterious icy oceans, where it's so cold the sea freezes.

I'm a **beluga whale** and I'm a very good singer.

White beluga whales live in the Arctic Ocean and sing so sweetly they are known as "sea canaries."

Weedy sea dragons live in kelp forests of the Southern Ocean. These dragons are actually fish—and it's the dads that look after the babies until they are ready to hatch from their eggs!

I've got a place on my belly where I keep eggs safe!

14

Eeeeek! Swim away!

I'm coming for you!

Polar bears are great swimmers, and deadly predators. They can hear a seal swimming 3 feet (1 meter) below thick ice!

I'm a narwhal. I can use my tooth to whack a fish.

The longest tooth in the world belongs to a male narwhal. He has only two teeth, but one of them can grow to 10 feet (3 meters) long. People used to think that narwhals' teeth came from unicorns!

Down to the deep

Are you scared of the dark? There are some strange animals in the inky-black deep sea.

Viperfish don't mind the dark because they can make their own light! They dangle a light in front of their face and swallow up the curious fish that come to investigate.

Did you know?

Sunlight passes through seawater, and helps the plants that live there to grow. Below 3,000 feet (914 meters) there is no light at all and the sea becomes a dark, cold, and scary place.

I'm a viperfish. Here, fishy fishy!

I'm a giant isopod.

Giant isopods look like huge woodlice. They can grow to 14 inches (35 centimeters) long and use their long feelers to find their way in the dark.

Vampire squid have huge eyes and they can make their whole body shimmer with light to scare other animals away.

Ooh, I'm SO scary!

Wow!

If you tried to live in the deep sea, you'd find the weight of water above you is so great that you'd be crushed to a pulp!

A gulper eel has such a big mouth it can swallow animals bigger than itself.

GULP!

In some places, hot water and gases escape from under the seabed and bubble into the sea. Weird, freaky animals, like hairy-clawed yeti crabs, live in these hotspots!

snip snip!

17

Coral reefs

Did you know that coral reefs are big enough to be seen from space?

There's a carnival of color in a coral reef! It makes a perfect home for billions of animals that find places to hide and hunt in the shadows.

I'm a regal angelfish.

I'm a porcupine fish.

I'm a blue tang.

We need sunlight and clean, salty water to grow.

Wow!

The Great Barrier Reef of Australia is actually a collection of about 3,000 reefs and 1,000 islands that are spread over 1,500 miles (2,400 kilometers) in the Coral Sea. It's the largest living structure on Earth.

I'm a parrot fish.

I'm a seahorse.

I'm a mandarin fish.

Corals become different shapes and colors as they grow. Brain coral look like brains, fan corals look like fans, and lettuce corals look like . . . can you guess?

Did you know?

A coral reef may be huge, but it's built by tiny animals that are no bigger than a fingernail! These animals are called polyps (say POL-ips) and they build rocky cups to sit in.

Ocean giants

The seas are home to some super-sized animals. They can be super speedy too!

Blue whales are so big that a whole one has never been weighed. A blue whale's poop is pink and longer than a person!

I'm the **biggest** creature **on Earth!**

The creepy-crawly Japanese spider crab has very long legs. It measures 146 inches (370 centimeters) from one side to the other.

Big mouth!

The world's biggest fish is the gentle whale shark. It's so large you could sit in its mouth!

I can live to 100 years old!

Wow!

Have you noticed how easy it is to float in seawater? It's denser, or thicker, than freshwater and that means it can support heavy bodies like these ocean giants.

My tusks are still growing!

Weighty walruses lumber slowly on the ice, but they are sleek swimmers underwater. They use their huge tusks to pull themselves back onto ice or land.

"Eye" can see you! This colossal squid has huge eyes—each one is as big as a dinner plate!

open wide!

I'm a colossal squid
and I can grow to 33 feet
(10 meters) long.

Giant clams live around coral reefs where there is so much food they can grow to be 3 feet (1 meter) wide, and can live for 100 years.

Meet the sharks

Great white sharks are fast, furious hunters— but not all sharks are scary!

This shortfin mako is the world's fastest shark, speeding through the water like a blue bullet at 50 miles (80 kilometers) an hour.

I'm super speedy!

Wow!

Shark skeletons are made of cartilage, which is a bit bendier than normal bone. Your nose and ears can bend because they have cartilage in them.

Wow!

Sharks' skin is covered in thousands of scales that are made of super-strong enamel— just like your teeth!

Humans? Yuk! No thanks!

Great whites are huge, fast, and clever sharks that mostly hunt fish and seals. They don't really like the taste of humans . . . that's a relief!

Why do hammerheads have such weird heads? This strange shape works like an airplane wing, helping a hammerhead shark change direction quickly.

I'm a hammerhead shark. I can see all around—even behind.

Get in my belly!

Basking sharks have huge mouths for gulping down lots of tiny sea creatures. They have 1,500 teeth, but they are harmless to people.

can you see me?

Wobbegong sharks are so well camouflaged among seaweed and stones that they can lie on the seabed and just wait until a fish swims close by. Then it's snap, gobble, swallow!

23

Coastal capers

Not all ocean creatures live in the sea. Take a look at the animals who like life above the water.

Penguins surf...

Penguins waddle on land but they are sleek swimmers and surfers in the sea! They use the waves to help them leap onto land.

Surf's up everyone—Let's play!

Wind power!

Waves are caused by wind. It whips up water at the top of the sea, turning it into a frothy white wave, especially at the coast.

Marine iguanas dive...

These reptiles live on land, but they swim to the seabed where they nibble on seaweed.

Wake up! it's time for Lunch!

Dolphins leap and spin . . .

Leaping out of the water helps dolphins avoid the jaws of a hungry shark. They also seem to leap just for the fun of it!

Catch me if you can!

Petrels plummet . . .

Petrels and other seabirds almost seem to fall out of the sky as they dive into the water and grab a tasty shrimp snack.

Fancy a dance?

Male blue-footed boobies are big show-offs. They march and dance on the shore so females can admire their lovely blue feet!

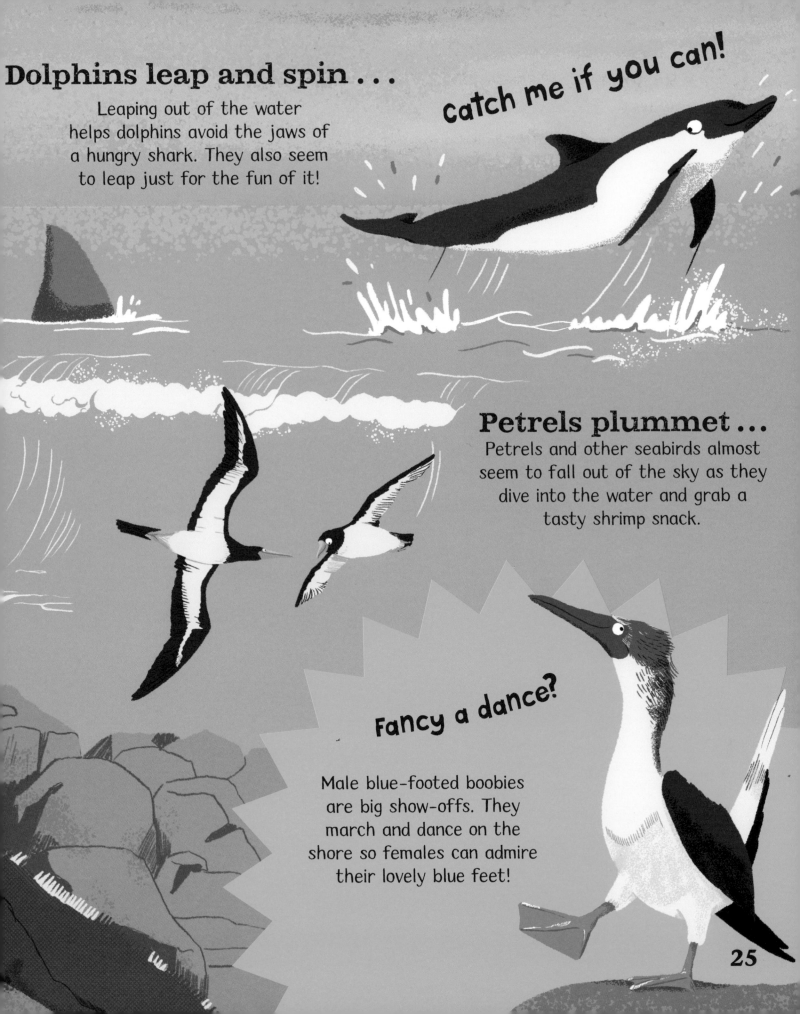

Freaky sea creatures

Which is the strangest animal in the sea? You decide!

Burp!

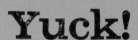

I'm a tentacled terror with super suckers!

Yuck!

Hagfish look like gross, slimy worms, but they have a toothy mouth that bites chunks of flesh from their victims. They even swim into another animal's mouth and eat it from the inside. That's revolting!

A cuttlefish has eight arms for grabbing prey and two tentacles. It has three hearts that pump blue blood and it can change color in a flash!

Munch crunch!

Most starfish have five arms, but a crown-of-thorns starfish can have 20! It nibbles at coral and has damaged large parts of the Great Barrier Reef.

The largest jellyfish are bigger than an adult, and they have long tentacles that are covered in nasty stingers.

I'm not a fish and I'm not made of jelly!

Wow!

Sea sponges don't have heads, hearts, eyes, legs, brains, or even mouths—but they have been around for more than 600 million years!

SNIP SNAP!

Crabs like to arm wrestle! Males grow one huge claw that they use to wave at their enemies, and if the threat doesn't work, they fight instead.

Scary seas

Meet some ocean killers with special skills. Don't get too near these creatures!

A blue-ringed octopus is smaller than a tennis ball, but its venom is strong enough to kill a person.

I'm small but deadly!

Wow!

Venom is poison that an animal uses to kill or injure another animal. Many ocean animals use spines or teeth to inject their venom.

stay away!

Scary stonefish are difficult to see on the seabed, but they have venom in their 13 spines—and they can still sting once they are dead!

Roarrrr!

Lionfish look lovely with their colorful stripes—but they are crafty killers. When a lionfish is scared, it raises its spines and stabs an attacker with a nasty dose of venom.

Mantis shrimps can punch their prey with such force they can break glass, or kill a crab in less than a second.

I'm a mantis shrimp and I'm really strong!

Wow!

Seashells can look harmless, but nasty nippers can live inside! Cone shells fire a poisoned harpoon at their prey. The venom is deadly to people!

Slithering sea snakes have some of the deadliest venom in the world. Thankfully, they are shy and swim away from people.

SSSSSSS!

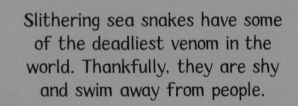

29

Ocean adventure

There are lots of fun and exciting ways to explore the ocean!

Surfing is so much fun that some dogs like to do it too! If they fall off their boards, it's easy for dogs to get back to shore—they doggy paddle, of course!

Did you know?

Plastiki is a boat made of 12,500 plastic bottles! It was sailed from the United States of America to Australia to help people learn how plastic is damaging the ocean.

I must be barking mad to do this!

More people have been to the Moon than the deepest part of the ocean!

Humans explore the deep sea in special vessels called submersibles. In 1960, two men traveled more than 6 miles (10 kilometers) down. They were surprised to find some little red shrimp living there!

You can explore under the ocean waves using a snorkel or scuba gear. Snorkels are breathing tubes that connect your mouth to the air above, but scuba divers take tanks of air down with them.

Don't try this at home!

I use my hands to "talk" underwater.

Wow!

Freedivers swim deep without taking any air with them. They can hold their breath for more than 20 minutes, but it's a very dangerous sport!

The world's biggest cruise ship takes more than 5,000 people on vacation. Once on board, they can enjoy 24 swimming pools, a giant slide, an skating rink, and an open-air theater!

swim, slide, eat—repeat!

Save our seas!

Our beautiful oceans are in trouble. How can we help?

Lots of our plastic waste ends up in the oceans, where it damages the animals that live there.

Use less plastic, and ALWAYS recycle it!

Wow!

13 million tons of plastic get into the oceans every year. Turtles often mistake plastic bags for jellyfish and die when they try to eat them.

Turtles lay their eggs on beaches and, once hatched, baby turtles crawl down to the sea. Beaches covered in litter make it very difficult for the baby turtles to find their way to the water.

Let's go swimming!

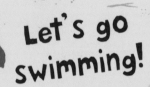

We burn fossil fuels, such as oil and gas, to heat our homes and travel in cars— but that's making the oceans too warm.

I'm walking to school

Going GREEN can SAVE our blue planet!